praise for
life, and everything in between

A delightfully charming book full of light, love and wry poetic aphorisms. Stephen Dodds obviously relishes being alive and wants to share his enjoyment with everyone.

—*Tony Ellis, author of There is Wisdom in Walnuts: 27 Poems by Tony Ellis and a Couple by his Dad.*

This book is highly original. Much of Dodds work is pregnant with metaphor and the author's tone is soothing, simple and free. His voice is crystal clear. His words have excellent rhythm. The artistry of the lines is wonderfully visual, spiritual, and sensual at times, when the author is steeped in his natural philosophical passions.

—*Rodney Charles*
Best Selling Author

"What touched me most was the pure honesty in Dodds' words. I was captivated and drawn into his world. A terrific read from beginning to end."

—*Daniel Jovkovic, Founder,*
Empty Heart.com - Youth Outreach

"life, and everything in between is an enjoyable ride….from light hearted to deeply emotional. Dodds is a skilled wordsmith who cleverly crafts images that touch our heart. Thank you for a gift both beautiful and profound."

—*Dennis Walsh, President & CEO Dennis Walsh & Associates*
Author & Motivational Speaker

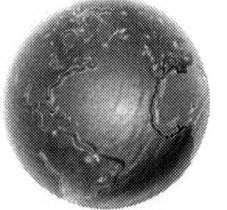

life,
and
everything
in between

Stephen J. Dodds

life,
and
everything
in between

Stephen J. Dodds

life, and everything in between

STEPHEN J. DODDS

© Stephen J. Dodds 2005

Published by 1stWorld Publishing
1100 North 4th St. Suite 131, Fairfield, Iowa 52556
tel: 641-209-5000 • fax: 641-209-3001
web: www.1stworldpublishing.com

First Edition

LCCN: 2005936455

SoftCover ISBN: 1595409750

HardCover ISBN: 1595409777

eBook ISBN: 1595409769

All rights reserved. No part of this book may be reproduced or utilized in any form or by any means, electronic or mechanical, including photocopying or recording, or by any information storage and retrieval system, without permission in writing from the author.

This material has been written and published solely for educational purposes. The author and the publisher shall have neither liability or responsibility to any person or entity with respect to any loss, damage or injury caused or alleged to be caused directly or indirectly by the information contained in this book.

The characters and events described in this text are intended to entertain and teach rather than present an exact factual history of real people or events.

contents one

doodles 3
melting pot 5
awakening 7

one way 11
life 13
jigsaw 15

no escape 19
regret me not 21
altered states 23

anointed sinner 27
and justice for all 29
lost 31

the boxer 35
north of superior 37
daydreams 39

contents two

respect 43
musical chairs 45
lucky man 47

free ride 51
stale ale 53
kids today 55

frequent flyer 59
teacups & popsicles 61
evil spirits 63

unpleasantly plump 67
poppycock 69
persona non gratis 71

autumn 75
another's dream 77
the bath 79

*life,
and
everything
in between*

dedication

For my Dad, who taught me it's never too late to change, for my Mom who always knew I would reach for the stars, for my brothers who adopted this only child, and for Alexandra who joins me on this wonderful ride called life.

2443—14327

Finally, to the staff on the 14th Floor, Princess Margaret Hospital, Toronto, one and all. Your professionalism and your compassion are total. We are forever grateful for the kindness and the care you provided our dad. You are sent from heaven.

first thoughts

Look at me. I can't believe I'm forty-four. Sometimes it seems like only yesterday I was riding my bike across Lakeshore, past the Red Barn, lacrosse stick in hand, on route to Les' house, playing chicken with the streetcars along the way. Damn, how time flies.

Funny enough I have no idea why I chose to share this meaningless fact with you, especially given you likely haven't a clue who I am, never mind who Les is, or where the Red Barn was located for that matter. And, I'm quite sure you really don't care. But that's okay.

You see it dawned on me a few months ago that I have so much to be thankful for. Not in terms of riches or fame, but more in terms of realizing that life is really what we make of it, and, equally important, who we choose to share it with. It's not about summarizing years gone by but rather cherishing each memory, regardless of how small or how silly, how good or how bad. It's about riding the ride, sometimes cautious but mostly with reckless abandon.

And that's what made me decide to write this book. A book I call, "life, and everything in between". A book that's really for me and for those I care most about. A book of emotions and feelings—some personal, some well thought out, most topical, and a few, quite simply pulled squarely from the hole in my $%#@!

So be warned, I have absolutely no formal training or experience where writing is concerned. Nor do I profess to be "expert" in any of the topics I write about …personal ones aside. On the contrary, all I offer is a mind full of "doodles" that I wish to share—nothing more and nothing less, just everything in between.

So, if it's Shakespeare or James Joyce you're after, I might not be for you. On the other hand, if you're in the mood for something fresh and real, even surreal perhaps, then please give me a look. I might surprise you… better yet, you might just surprise yourself.

After all, we only live once, so let's seize the moment. I did, and now I have a book with my picture on the cover. And, that my friend, blows my mind… "Who'd have thunk it."

*"I skate to where the puck is going to be,
not where it has been."*

*"You'll always miss 100%
of the shots you don't take."*

*Wayne Gretzky
The Great One #99*

"Let your imagination release your imprisoned possibilities."

—Dr. Robert H. Schuller
Minister, Crystal Cathedral

doodles

Thoughts appear
like renderings in my mind
given life
only when released
to the clean white page
Always changing in form and function
resembling the theme
only by chance
No agenda to follow
nor rules to maintain
The only competition
between the lines
No time limits
some delays
No rhyme, nor reason
Just words forming pictures
from the doodles in my mind

"Our true nationality is man-kind."

—*H.G. Wells*
Author & Historian (1866—1946)

melting pot

I've seen the world
and reveled in its complexity
Broad cultures
of vivid colors dot the globe
A melting pot of the rich, the poor,
the gay, the straight
the bad, the good, the purple the green
the healthy and the weak
the old, the young
Each simple ingredients
simmering as one
A cornucopia of flavors for all to share
What a monochromatic world it must be
for the prudish and the narrow minded
landlocked in self preservation
ignorant to change
I'm so thankful I am different
I hope you are different
In life, we all are different
Embrace it

"Welcome every morning with a smile.
Look on the new day as another
special gift from your creator,
another golden opportunity to complete
what you were unable to finish yesterday.
Be a self starter.
Let your first hour set the theme
of success and positive action
that is certain to echo through your entire day.
Today will never happen again.
Don't waste it with a false start
or no start at all.
You were not born to fail."

—Og Mandino
Essayist & Psychologist (1923—1996)

awakening

Lawn dew glistens
peacefully silent
as the morning mist
drifts between land and sky
All is still
Slowly the sun rises
blanketing the horizon
with a soft yellow glow
A robin's song
welcomes the dawn
of another day
to savor
life

> "The church says the earth is flat,
> but I know that it is round,
> for I have seen the shadow on the moon,
> and I have more faith in a shadow
> than in a church."
>
> —Ferdinand Magellan
> Explorer (480—1521)

one way

Frustration lies rooted in the nay Sayer's mind
without worry of consequence
Nourished by an arsenal of non objectivity
transposed into a dialect few can comprehend
Blocked passages forge an obstacle course
only the negative can navigate
Suggestions appear in bright red text
disguised as stop signs along the way
Dead end streets and narrow alleys
form the landscape that ends where it begins
unchanged and unexplored
The enemy speeds by in opposite directions
opting for a left turn at the fork in the road
Steadfast the stubborn rider
stays the course on the vanilla highway
determined to press ahead alone
Leaving confusion in his wake

*"I hear and I forgot.
I see and I remember.
I do and I understand."*

—*Confucius*
Philosopher (551 BC—479 BC)

life

In a flash
the world can disappear
without warning
History solidifying the past
Today a forgone conclusion
Tomorrow uncertain
The choice is ours
in this game
called life
Do, help or watch
We can
reach for the stars
and seize the moment
or simply exist
and wait on fate
For life is a gift without instruction
Result, certain
The doer leaves a mark
The helper, a footnote at best
The watcher, forgotten
Choose wisely and soar to the heavens
No regrets

"We are all apprentices in a craft where no one ever becomes a master."

—Ernest Hemingway
Writer (1898—1961)

jigsaw

Random thoughts adorn the page
like a jig saw
connecting not in context
but adjoining perfectly
in concert
A dysfunctional melody
of syllables and nouns
The corner pieces
a montage of broken sentences
the picture itself
a naked pallet
for the imaginative mind
The story yet untold
laden with hidden agenda
coming together in a symphony
for the soul
With no pieces missing
the puzzle is complete

"Oh what a tangled web we weave, when first we practice to deceive!"

Sir Walter Scott
Historian (1771—1832)

no escape

The puppet master and the spider
control their space
without fear or regret
The intended prey
courted
by webbed strings
seduced
with false promises
captured
by fate
A predetermined conclusion
with no way out

"Every day you make progress.
Every step may be fruitful.
Yet there will stretch out before you
and ever-lengthening, ever-ascending,
ever-improving path.
You know you will never get
to the end of this journey.
But this, so far from discouraging,
only adds to the joy
and glory of the climb."

Sir Winston Churchill
British Politician (1874—1965)

regret me not

Clouds surround me searching for light
The sun hides in the shadows
as the wind counts to ten
The rain waiting in the wings
for thunder to lead the way
A game of tag
that only nature can win
Winter asleep for the season
Fall a distant memory
We trade parkas for wind breakers
shovels for trowels
Sewing seeds for a tomorrow not yet here
Living for the future
while missing the pleasures of today
Smell the roses before they wilt
Replace regrets
with fond memories
After all
we live but once

"And so, my fellow Americans:
ask not what your country can do—
but what you can do
for your country.

My fellow citizens of the world:
ask not what America will do for you,
but what together we can do
for the freedom of man."

John F. Kennedy
President, United States of America '61–'63
(1917—1963)

altered states

I marvel at the hypocrisy
of the non voting patriot
Free to leave their mark
yet unwilling to exercise this privilege
Able to watch censored TV
or listen to time-delayed airwaves
yet void of complaint
Ignorant of the ability
to switch channels
looking instead to Big Brother
for guidance
Prostituting themselves
with empty ballots
while chairing
water cooler debates
How misguided they are
to ridicule the foreign society
as they dwell
in their altered states
Claiming to be united

"But, good my brother, do not,
as some ungracious pastors do.
Show me the steep and thorny way
to heaven whilst like a puffed and
reckless libertine himself,
the primrose path of dalliance
treads and wrecks not his own."

William Shakespeare
Playwright (1566—1616)

anointed sinner

The kind gesture of the stranger
is awarded
with cynicism and mistrust
The irony festers like an open sore
devoid of feeling
Like a virus
contagious to all who witness
Benign to only the few
who graciously acknowledge
the out held hand
Sunday morning television fills the airwaves
The weak held captive in the anointed hour
Promises of life ever lasting
traded for the offering
The simple minded stay tuned
The tailored preachers rejoice
The stranger on the street alone
still hungers

"Imagine there's no countries,
it isn't hard to do;
nothing to kill or die for,
and no religion too.
Imagine all the people living life in peace."

John Lennon
Musician (1940—1980)

and justice for all

The world changed forever that tragic September day
Our freedom turned upside down
A victim of hate
Our guts ached
as the horror of the ashy darkness
rose from the innocent grave
once guarded by towering pride
CNN bombarded our senses in real time
No delayed Beirut rerun
too often dismissed
Tears of a nation
were unable to wash away the pain
indelibly inscribed in our very core
Far away the guttersnipe assassin
burrowed in his cave
Sending his brother's sons to proffer his cowardly deed
All in the name of a God he can't possibly know
So we heal and rebuild
as the carrion eater rots in misery
Afraid to meet his Allah
for fear the truth will then be told

*"Pain is temporary.
It may last a minute,
or an hour,
or a day,
or a year.
But eventually it will subside
and something else will take its place.
If I quit however,
it lasts forever."*

Lance Armstrong
Cyclist

lost

Boys at thirty-five
Socially disenfranchised
Trying in vain to escape responsibility
Directionless
Unchallenged as children
they grew wild
No roots of their own
So still they play games
Mom and Dad to sustain them
on life's free ride
Pride their only fare
In a child's bed they sleep alone
Crying for help
with no place to hide
Too tired to try
Fearing a tomorrow
that always arrives too soon
Parents shamefully mistaking
hand outs for love
All the while
life passes them by

*"I have been wounded but not yet slain.
I shall lie here and bleed awhile.
Then I shall rise up and fight again."*

*Vince Lombardi
Football Coach (1913—1970)*

the boxer

Round eleven
the crowd on their feet
The brave contender sits on his stool exhausted
Salty sweat pools below
The cut man
presses the iced flat iron
to the slit that was once an eye
He summons the energy
to gulp another breath
his cheeks too swollen to grimace
Vaseline smears his beaten face
yet he lumbers to his feet for the final round
His hands hang like dead weights
alongside his rippled torso
He steels himself for three minutes of hell
knowing he needs a knockout
The champion waits at the center of the ring
A flurry follows
Looking up from the canvas respectful
as the referee counts to ten
Quitting was never an option

"Nature gives to every time and season
some beauties of its own;
and from morning to night,
as from the cradle to the grave,
it is but a succession of changes
so gentle and easy that
we can scarcely mark their progress."

Charles Dickens
Novelist (1812—1870)

north of superior

In the jump seat of the Otter
I gaze at the majesty of the great white north
The land as far as the eye can see
tattooed with lakes of green and blue
Antlers appear below
as a bull moose swims to the far shore
Brown bear cubs wait their turn
as waves splash at their paws
A beaver stakes her claim on the rocky bank
proudly constructing her gnawed tree abode
decorated in birch bark, and sewn with forest vine
Bait fish dance in unison
marking the glassy surface with rippled rings
playing hide n seek with the sun
The loon's song the only sound heard
in this unspoiled land
I still call home

*"Those who dream by day
are cognizant of many things
which escape those who only dream by night."*

*Edgar Allen Poe
Writer (1809—1849)*

daydreams

The surreal landscape floats effortlessly on a canvas
A mish mash of textures
The rain stops for a brief moment
as a ribbon of color blankets the clear blue sky
The fly that was trapped behind the screen
sits patiently awaiting his escape
while the kettle refuses to boil
Amused you realize that the light of day
is in fact a news clip from a yesterday long past
You are joyous and free
as you close your mind for the season
Visions of tomorrow dance in your head
Fond memories of a lullabies soothing tale
You look down to see that your sandals are damp
from the sands of time
Without warning you awake
to the sounds of laughter
Was it a dream
or had reality taken a strange twist

> "Stevie son,
> I gave it my best shot."

Tommy Dodds
Dad, Milwright (1932—2000)

respect

It was '64, I was three
I remember a sweets shop
at the foot of the bank
cobble stone streets, row houses
and, my Nana
We left Newcastle that year
Canada bound
Me with a Beatles haircut
The Atlantic our rite of passage
How brave my parents were
to leave everything behind
Three Geordies, with only each other
the clothes on our backs, and a few pounds sterling
Dad's hardened hands and Mom's iron will
In search of a better life
for me, their only son
Many years passed before returning to England
Proudly, I recall dad's tears
as we settled into the first class cabin
aboard the BA jumbo jet
Our family intact
enroute to the Corner House
Looking back, how ironic it was
that they thanked me
for their tickets home

"There is more treasure in books than in all the pirate's loot on Treasure Island—and best of all, you can enjoy these riches every day of your life."

Walt Disney
Cartoonist (1901—1966)

musical chairs

Eloquently connected sonnets
create a kaleidoscope of pastel colors
each of varying shapes and sizes
Divorced from reality
the words float free
Unencumbered by rules
Lost in a game
of musical chairs
The pages spring to life
opening a Pandora's Box
filled with mystery and illusion
You savor each delicious moment
yearning for the unexpected
left exhausted wanting more
But, there is no conclusion
to the never ending story

"Love is patient; love is kind.
Love is not envious
or boastful or arrogant or rude.
It does not insist on its own way.
It is not irritable or resentful;
it does not rejoice in wrong doing,
but rejoices in truth.
Love bears all things,
believes all things,
hopes all thing,
and endures all things.
And now faith, hope and love abide,
and the greatest of these is love."

The Bible
I Corinthians 13: 5 - 9

lucky man

She dances through life
with the grace of an angel
Sculpted and sassy
her contagious smile
radiates from deep within
shining like a beacon
Exuding confidence
yet intentionally subdued
she is spectacular in the simplest of ways
Her beauty only trumped
by her unbridled spirit
Her heart overflows with kindness
transcending generations and social standing
She dissolves tears into laughter, sorrow into joy
Always passionate, forever gracious
She is my chosen ally
My sword in battle and my shield in retreat
Loved by all
but by none more than me
She completes me
Alexandra
My wife my life

*"Coming together is a beginning,
staying together is progress,
and working together is success."*

Henry Ford
Industrialist (1863 –1947)

free ride

The unencumbered relationship
or a free ride to no where
Like the directionless subway
in life's dead end tunnel
A recipe full of missing ingredients
that fills the belly
with false satisfaction
An empty belonging
in a purposeless journey
with no beginning nor end
Just long pauses
to fill the gaps
Successfully yet incompletely
Two halves
Not,
together as one

"Well, you see Norm, it's like this—a herd of buffalo can only move as fast as the slowest buffalo. And, when the herd is hunted, it is the lowest and weakest ones at the back that are killed first. This natural selection is good for the heard as a whole, because the general speed and health of the whole group keeps improving by the regular killing of the weakest members. In much the same way, the human brain can only operate as fast as the slowest brain cells. Now, as we know, excessive intake of alcohol kills brain cells. But naturally it attacks the slowest and weakest brain cells first. In this way, regular consumption of beer eliminates the weaker brain cells, making the brain a more faster and efficient machine. And, that Norm is why you always feel smarter after a few beers."

Cliff Clavin
Fictional television character,
Cheers (1982—1993)

stale ale

They called it the Almont
It sat alone on the corner
An old gray building in need of repair
with dimly lit smoke filled rooms
and a simple menu
of draft, stubby bottled beers
and whiskey by the shot
Home to the toothless and the tobacco-stained
the salesman and the retired whore
the factory worker and the unemployed
Thirst their only friend
Regrets the common thread
Tales of yesterdays past and boasts of tomorrow
their anthem
Lyrics fueled with liquid courage
Yet garbled by faded memory
All the while
the children played outside
Stoic and hardened
Experiencing life

"Life would be infinitely happier if we could only be born at the age of eighty and gradually approach eighteen."

Mark Twain
Writer (1835—1910)

kids today

How hypocritical adults are
to ridicule the child's identity
We, such popular fools in our day
adorned in platform shoes
and long feathered hair
Our tie-dyed world complete
with bell bottoms and disco
Filling prescriptions
at the study hall pharmacy
Losing days in a Pink Floyd haze
Doing the fashion two-step
when punk became the rage
Hello
Today's teens are a reflection of who we were
Simply in different costume
And, they will be us again
just as we became
our parents

"Once I had breakfast in Germany,
lunch in Switzerland,
dinner in Italy
and I slept in France,
all in one day…
or something like that"

Doddsy
Joan & Tom's kid

frequent flyer

A fancy hotel greets
the weary traveler
with crisp white sheets
and panoramic views
Room service arrives
with no reservations required
Alone bedside
he dines for one
on toasted club and rum and coke
His wrinkled body copes
as his mind calibrates today's time zone
Morning dissolves into night
afternoon a passing blur
With another flight tomorrow
he now rests
In his new room
he calls home for the night

"Imagination is more important then knowledge.
Knowledge is limited.
Imagination encircles the world."

Albert Einstein
Scientist (1879—1955)

teacups & popsicles

Once in a while
the sun and clouds converge
into a sea of muted tones
Not bright nor dreary
just somewhere in between
Then you ponder
a silly fact
porcupines and elephants
are so very different
Feeling hungry and tired
you crave for the unknown
but settle for your quiet daydream
Friends arrive
carrying tea cups and popsicles
Yet another simple coincidence
or a well earned lazy trance

"The wine urges me on,
the bewitching wine,
which sets even a wise man to singing
and to laughing gently and
rouses him up to dance
and brings forth words
which were better unspoken."

Homer
Philosopher (800 BC—700 BC)

evil spirits

Forgive me
I fear I have inherited
the fool's thirst
That insatiable desire
for just one more
Passed down from father to son
Transforming
hero to villain
comic to fool
One ounce at a time
A selfish frolic
seldom planned and usually fun
Too often regretted
And
at times disgraceful
My evil spirits
in their glass houses
Offering
nowhere to hide
the bottled up madness
of being me

"If it weren't for the fact that
the TV set and the refrigerator are so far apart,
some of us wouldn't get
any exercise at all."

Joey Adams
Comedian, Author, Columnist
(1911—1999)

unpleasantly plump

Look what we've become, this super sized state
Complete with drive through parents, their kids in tow
Dining a la carte
on large fries and Krispy Kreme
Yet we wonder why the child's belly grows
Sitting in a remote control world
where Xbox and Game Boys rule
Baseball diamonds and bicycles retired to pasture
while the flat screen child minder sits idle
spewing fast food propaganda
between Springer reruns and adult cartoons
A place where fresh air is replaced by AC
and pick up football is played over the internet
with Big Gulp in hand
So shamefully sad
So painfully true

"I have been impressed with the urgency of doing. Knowing is not enough we must apply; being willing is not enough; we must do."

Leonardo da Vinci
Renaissance Artist (1452—1519)

poppycock

Shattered glass, like broken promises
are not quick fixes
The solution while easily found
not so easily applied
Give and take must coincide
without unilateral opinion
or the nexus of evil will take root
Climbing the ladder to reason
is akin to swimming in a sea of uncertainty
Both roads will lead you to a location
but neither guarantees a successful conclusion
It's the unexplored path
that uplifts the spirit
Carrying you to new heights
Settling for less, will leave you in a quagmire
void of self worth
over taken with fruitless abandon
Well wishes and good intentions
are just that
poppycock

"Most people are other people.
Their thoughts are someone else's opinions,
their lives a mimicry,
their passions a quotation."

Oscar Wilde
Poet, Novelist & Dramatist
(1854—1900)

persona non gratis

Embark with me
on this road called life
Discover the inner you
Uncloak those hidden treasures
trapped beneath
that guarded persona
Set your spirit free
let your inhibitions run wild
Open up your world
to the wonders of your mind
And your mind
to the wonders of the world
For freedom is a journey
born from within
Never stagnant, often peaceful
Forever purposeful
Love yourself
so the world may see
who you are
not who you want to be

"It was, as I have said, a fine Autumnal day; the sky was clear and serene, and nature wore that rich and golden livery which we always associate with the idea of abundance. The forest had put on their sober brown and yellow, while some trees of the tender kind had been nipped by the frosts into brilliant dyes of oranges, purple and scarlet."

Washington Irving
Historian (1783—1859)

autumn

One smell of the forest
tells you its autumn
The gentle breeze hints
snow will soon follow
The crisp clean air
just cold enough
to don your woolly sweater
The trees surge to life
against the pale blue sky
A portrait of golden yellows and reds
Standing proud like soldiers
before bunking down
for a long winter's nap
Their fallen leaves
prepare their beds and warm their roots
Songs emerge from the branches
while squirrels scurry to collect acorns
for their treasure chest
The fall is alive in nature's splendor
Walk with me

"Sit in reverie and watch the changing color of the waves that break upon the idle seashore of the mind."

Henry Wadsworth Longfellow
Poet (1807—1882)

another's dream

The staircase winds upward toward the sky
as the tranquility of time ticks away the fleeting moments
pausing just long enough
to escape the thunderous echo sure to follow
The contorted figurine that lies lazily on the horizon
now casts her shadow in all directions
Calling out to no one
she is focused in your gaze
The rain falls as you ponder life's journey
wondering aloud if you are alone in your thoughts
The answer to follow is silence
Yet another unanswered prayer
Only then do you realize the inevitable
As you awake
from someone else's dream

"I like nonsense—
it wakes up the brain cells.
Fantasy is a necessary ingredient in living.
It's a way of looking at life through
the wrong end of a telescope—
and that enables you to laugh at
all of life's realities."

Dr. Seuss
Writer & Illustrator (1904—1991)

the bath

It's times like these
when the thoughts of butterflies and prickly bushes
play havoc with your mind
A senseless illusion of ferries and bats
Dancing in unison
adorned with grape leaves and figs
Your eye flutters, then
in an instant you awake
to the smells of cinnamon and taffy
Bubbles guard you from harm
as you embark on a journey like no other
No longer trapped in a wasteland of despair
Warm and wrinkled
you realize that the world is indeed your oyster
The water drains from the tub
oblivious to your thoughts or feelings
Suspended in time
you relax your mind
Soaking, wondering, feeling
life
And, everything in between

after thoughts

I was just wrapping up the final touches of this book when we received the news that my father in law had been diagnosed with (AML) Acute Myeloid Leukemia. Needless to say we were devastated.

Within days Dad would be sent to Princess Margaret Hospital in Toronto to commence treatment. It was there that we first met Ray. Ray too had been diagnosed with AML and had just finished his first round of radical chemotherapy. A French Canadian, Ray is half Dad's age and then some. Now, Nick "the Greek" would be Ray's new roommate. What a combination, especially when you add the rest of our clan.

I say this because oddly enough Ray touched our lives in ways he may never understand. And, in some ways, I'm sure that we have touched his. You see, when we first arrived at the hospital Ray hadn't eaten in weeks. He couldn't stomach food. His stubbly head an obvious battle wound, his eyes bloodshot and tired. Yet regardless of circumstance, Ray's constant smile lit up the room.

Ray exuded positive energy. His cup always half full and never half empty, he was optimistic but not naïve, his dignity firmly intact and his hope unparalleled. Best of all Ray had a smile so big it was contagious — a winner in every single sense of the word. Ray was just the medicine that Dad needed.

Now, six days or so into Dad's chemotherapy Ray called me in California to tell me that he's going home for a few days. Oh, he knows that he'll be returning to hospital in a week's time but that's a future worry. Today Ray celebrates. Today, my family celebrates as well.

We celebrate for Ray, for Dad and yes, we celebrate for life …and everything in between.

Bon chance mon ami
Doddsy

what was I thinking

In case you were wondering, I thought it might be helpful to give you a little insight as to how the photos and the quotes tie into the random "doodles" I shared with you.

My goal was to express my feelings on a variety of topics, as honestly and as passionately as possible. I tried to evoke a sense of myself in each piece I wrote. To hammer my point home I solicited the help of others. That's where the quotes come in. I carefully selected each quote to best compliment my "two cents". After all, if they said it, it must be true. Well maybe not, but then again it's my book.

The same holds true with the photos I chose. Hopefully you will see a common theme. In short, live life to the fullest.

Collage of children—look at the smiling faces of the multi-cultural children around the world. Can't we all just get along —*melting pot*

Jigsaw pieces—life's all about making choices, and more important, about making them at the right time and the right place. Putting the pieces together, one by one—*jigsaw*

Chess pieces—life is like a game of chess …calculated and purposeful—*no escape*

Mask—far too often we hide behind a mask, refusing to accept the reality of life—*lost*

Boy on pond playing hockey—no worries, just a stick a puck and the frozen pond—*north of superior*

Man and women hand in hand—come on, this ones obvious—*lucky man*

Pocket watch—we only have one life to live so we must maximize the little time we have—*free ride*

Santorini, Greece—if there is a more magical place on the planet Earth, I haven't found it …yet—*frequent flyer*

Collage of man's facial expressions—hear no evil, see no evil, speak no evil …do nothing—*pleasantly plump*

Roulette wheel—I always wore #11 when I played hockey and lacrosse. It just seemed fitting that I find a way to include it —*autumn*

And that my friends, is all she wrote.

www.ingramcontent.com/pod-product-compliance
Lightning Source LLC
Chambersburg PA
CBHW072202100426
42738CB00011BA/2502